HOPPING ARCTIC HARES

THERESA EMMINIZER

PowerKiDS press™

New York

Published in 2022 by The Rosen Publishing Group, Inc.
29 East 21st Street, New York, NY 10010

Portions of this work were originally authored by Therese Shea and published as *Arctic Hares*. All new material in this edition authored by Theresa Emminizer.

Editor: Jill Keppeler
Book Design: Michael Flynn

Photo Credits: Cover, pp. 1, 11, 13 (inset) Robert Postma/Design Pics/Getty Images; (series background) Stefan Sorean/Shutterstock.com; p. 5 by wildestanimal/Moment Open/Getty Images; p. 7 Gabriel Gersch/Getty Images; p. 9 Chanonry/Shutterstock.com; p. 13 (main) Antero Topp/Shutterstock.com; pp. 15 (all), 19, 21 Paul Loewen/Shutterstock.com; p. 17 Posnov/Moment/Getty Images.

Library of Congress Cataloging-in-Publication Data

Names: Emminizer, Theresa, author.
Title: Hopping arctic hares / Theresa Emminizer.
Description: New York : PowerKids Press, [2022] | Series: Animals of the
    tundra | Includes index.
Identifiers: LCCN 2020020313 | ISBN 9781725326354 (library binding) | ISBN
    9781725326330 (paperback) | ISBN 9781725326347 (6 pack)
Subjects: LCSH: Arctic hare–Juvenile literature. | Tundra
    animals–Juvenile literature.
Classification: LCC QL737.L32 E47 2022 | DDC 599.32–dc23
LC record available at https://lccn.loc.gov/2020020313

Manufactured in the United States of America

Some of the images in this book illustrate individuals who are models. The depictions do not imply actual situations or events.

CPSIA Compliance Information: Batch #CSPK22. For Further Information contact Rosen Publishing, New York, New York at 1-800-237-9932.

Find us on

CONTENTS

Meet the Arctic Hare!

A hare is an animal that looks like a big rabbit. Arctic hares are the largest hares in North America. They're about 19 to 26 inches (48 to 66 cm) long. They weigh 6 to 15 pounds (2.7 to 6.8 kg).

A Tundra Home

Arctic hares live in the tundra. That's a place where few plants grow because the ground is frozen. **Temperatures** in the tundra are very low. The Arctic hare has special **adaptations** that help it **survive**.

Built to Survive

Arctic hares have thick fur to keep them warm. Their small body and short ears are built to hold in heat. Hares have long, flat feet that keep them from sinking into the snow. Long claws help them dig.

Arctic hares have great eyesight. Their eyes are placed on the sides of their head. This allows them to see all around without turning their head! Their long, black eyelashes act like sunglasses, shading their eyes.

A Coat to Match

During winter, an Arctic hare's fur is white, except for the tips of its ears, which are black. This **camouflage** helps it hide in the snow and ice. The fur turns brown or gray in summer to match its home.

Snacks for a Hare

Arctic hares use their powerful sense of smell to find moss underneath the snow. They also eat small sticks and berries. Arctic hares usually come out at night. They gather in large groups when they eat.

Arctic Hare Families

Female, or girl, Arctic hares make nests in the ground. They give birth to two to eight babies in springtime or early summer. Babies leave the nest when they're a few weeks old.

Staying Safe

Wolves, lynx, and Arctic foxes hunt Arctic hares. But Arctic hares have a great **defense**—they're superfast! Arctic hares have long, powerful legs. They can reach speeds up to 40 miles (64 km) per hour.

Small but Mighty

There's much more to Arctic hares than meets the eye. They're more than cute bunnies. They're strong survivors! With their speed, sharp eyesight, and strong sense of smell, Arctic hares are able to live in the **harsh** tundra.

Fancy Features

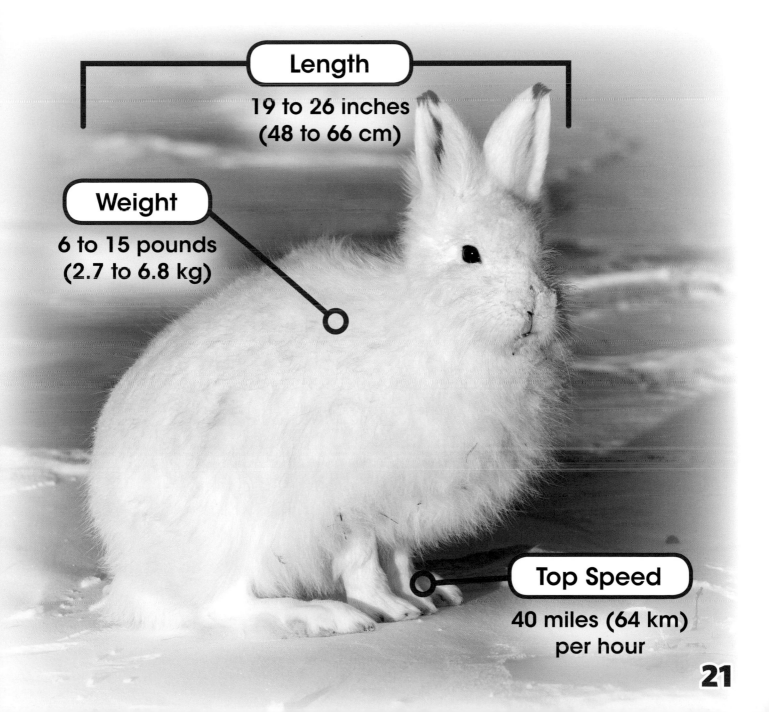

Length
19 to 26 inches
(48 to 66 cm)

Weight
6 to 15 pounds
(2.7 to 6.8 kg)

Top Speed
40 miles (64 km)
per hour

GLOSSARY

adaptation: Changes in a living thing that help it live better in its habitat, or home.

camouflage: Colors or shapes on animals that allow them to blend in with their surroundings.

defense: A feature of a living thing that helps it keep safe.

harsh: Difficult or unpleasant.

survive: To keep living.

temperature: How hot or cold something is.

FOR MORE INFORMATION

WEBSITES

Arctic Hare
www.nationalgeographic.com/animals/mammals/a/arctic-hare/
National Geographic presents this website full of information on the Arctic hare, including diet, size, and habitat.

Arctic Hare: *Lepus articus*
nhpbs.org/natureworks/arctichare.htm
View photos and learn more about Arctic hares on this PBS website.

BOOKS

Hansen, Grace. *Arctic Hare*. Minneapolis, MN: Abdo Kids, 2020.

Pettiford, Rebecca. *Arctic Hares*. Minneapolis, MN: Bellwether Media, 2019.

Publisher's note to parents and teachers: Our editors have reviewed the websites listed here to make sure they're suitable for students. However, websites may change frequently. Please note that students should always be supervised when they access the internet.

INDEX